BERND DEGEN

DISCUS
HOW TO BREED THEM

TRANSLATED BY HOWARD H. HIRSCHHORN

Distributed in the UNITED STATES by T.F.H. Publications, Inc., One T.F.H. Plaza, Neptune City, NJ 07753; in CANADA to the Pet Trade by H & L Pet Supplies Inc., 27 Kingston Crescent, Kitchener, Ontario N2B 2T6; Rolf C. Hagen Ltd., 3225 Sartelon Street, Montreal 382 Quebec; in CANADA to the Book Trade by Macmillan of Canada (A Division of Canada Publishing Corporation), 164 Commander Boulevard, Agincourt, Ontario M1S 3C7; in ENGLAND by T.F.H. Publications, The Spinney, Parklands, Portsmouth PO7 6AR; in AUSTRALIA AND THE SOUTH PACIFIC by T.F.H. (Australia) Pty. Ltd., Box 149, Brookvale 2100 N.S.W., Australia; in NEW ZEALAND by Ross Haines & Son, Ltd., 82 D Elizabeth Knox Place, Panmure, Auckland, New Zealand; in the PHILIPPINES by Bio-Research, 5 Lippay Street, San Lorenzo Village, Makati, Rizal; in SOUTH AFRICA by Multipet Pty. Ltd., Box 235, New Germany, South Africa 3620. Published by T.F.H. Publications, Inc. Manufactured in the United States of America by T.F.H. Publications, Inc.

TABLE OF CONTENTS

PHOTO CREDITS

Many, many people have helped me to properly illustrate this book. I sincerely hope I haven't forgotten anyone ... if I have, please forgive me. Without attempting to alphabetize or highlight any single photographer, since all are skilled and important, the following is a list of the photographers:

I took many of the photos, of course.
Dr. Herbert R. Axelrod
Dr. Eduard Schmidt-Focke
Burkhard Kahl
Arend v. d. Nieuwenhuizen
Fred Rosenzweig
Hans-Georg Petersmann
Dr. Clifford Chan
Osvaldo Gonzalez
R. Annunziata
Oliver Deutschle
Manfred Goebel
Lo Wing Yat
Hubert Kleykers
Hans Mayland
Teo Mee Ming
Emeran Pischvai
Jack Wattley
Mr. Heymans
J. Steffen
Andre Roth
Ruda Zukal
Thomas Horeman
Edward Taylor
Midori Shobo (Japan)
Marine Planning (Japan)
Harold Beck
Gene Wolfsheimer
Chuck Sanders
Alfred Castro

Preface

Writing a book on the discus fishes is certainly one of the most exciting tasks for a non-fiction writer who is dedicated to these creatures.

Even today, the discus is still called the king of aquarium fish, and rightly so. He's really regal—of majestic stature, he's also splendid in his coloration while being hard to care for, fastidious in his feeding habits and difficult to breed.

Much has already been written on the various discus fishes, and every hobbyist has his secret recipes. This book is meant to help the newcomer to discus

Even today discus are still called 'the king of the aquarium.'

Bernd Degen has written more books about discus than anyone else in the world. He is considered the world's leading discus authority.

The experienced discus aquarist will find a great deal of new information in this book.

Taken at the offices of TFH, from left to right: Jack Wattley, Dr. Herbert R. Axelrod, and the author, Bernd Degen.

aquaristics. The experienced discus aquarist, too, will find a great deal of new information in this book. No doubt one or another of my readers won't completely share my views, but I've successfully tested everything here over the last fifteen years of working with my discus, and it works for me.

I'd certainly be happy if this discus book makes new friends for these fish and helps their keepers give them the best possible home in their tanks.

History of an Aquarium King

It's hardly conceivable that our discus was described as early as 1840 by the Viennese ichthyologist Dr. Johann Jacob Heckel when you realize that German hobbyists, among the world's best, didn't come to really know it until after World War II. In 1959, Harald Schultz wrote the first extensive report on capturing discus.

Names of such people as Dr. Herbert R. Axelrod, U.S.A., and Dr. Eduard Schmidt-Focke, Germany, come up in discus literature and discussions because they are intensively involved with the discus, encouraging—with breeding and working out of the genetics of coloration—its greater familiarity among German

Bernd Degen with Dr. Eduard Schmidt-Focke. Dr. Schmidt-Focke is considered the father of the modern discus varieties in Europe.

Dr. Eduard Schmidt-Focke with an original painting in which he and Jack Wattley appear in a ghostly image among the discus.

The two grand old men of the discus world. Dr. Herbert R. Axelrod, left, has collected almost all of the color varieties and species in Brazil. One of the discus was named after him, *Symphysodon aequifasciata axelrodi*, the brown or red discus. He gave many of the discus to Dr. Eduard Schmidt-Focke, shown right. The two have been friends for more than 40 years.

aquarists. Ever more beautiful and intensively colored specimens are being bred from the modestly colored specimens captured in the wild. In Germany, Dr. Schmidt-Focke and the Reverend Schulten quickly developed discus into sought-after rarities. Jack Wattley of Fort Lauderdale, Florida made a name for himself through his turquoise discus, which quickly became known as the Wattley discus among other discus aquarists.

The victorious entry of this fish onto the aquarium scene was as if it had been programmed. The only problem that threatened to impede the appearance of this fish in many hobbyists' tanks was its cost. The various discus fishes were and still are very expensive. Furthermore, they are very demanding as to their care, water quality and diet, all of which guarantees that not everyone can just decide to raise some discus as a sideline. So this majestic creature has thus far been spared the fate that befell the angel fish, whose easy breeding rapidly led to its mass production in our tanks. Discus breeding is still so difficult that it is limited to serious aquarists—and that's a good thing.

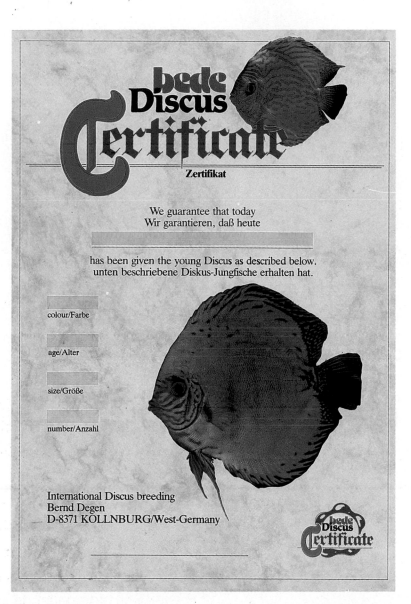

Certificates of authenticity are available from Bernd Degen. These certificates accompany sales of all his discus.

"If you flip through the ads in aquarium magazines you'll find many that offer discus for sale . . ."

Original basic breeding stocks, like this *Symphysodon aequifasciata haraldi*, were used to bring out the colors in the modern discus.

Discus in Germany Today

If you flip through the ads in aquarium magazines you'll find many that offer various sizes of discus for sale, which seems to indicate that there are enough successful discus breeders around. But that's not the case. The number of really successful breeders is much less than you're led to believe by seeing those ads. It's often only random success—and I believe that some people place ads for a whole year just to stay in touch with the world.

The demand for discus in West Germany remains larger than breeders can satisfy. Quality is wanted, and only quality lasts on the market. Brown and simply green fish can hardly be sold off anymore. All variations of turquoise discus are in demand, as well as the best royal blues and specimens with vibrant red coloration.

A new variety, which is not going to be a winner, is this hi-fin which lacks body coloration.

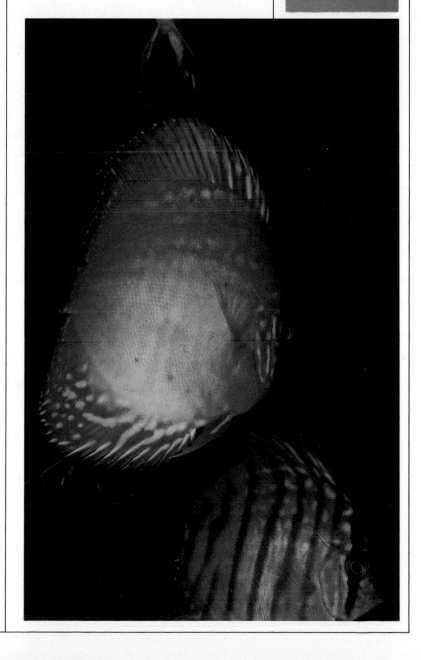

Inside the Degen fish hatchery are huge aquariums which contain discus ready for sale. The discus are sorted by size and variety.

The capture of wild specimens once meant a lot to discus enthusiasts. Large numbers were imported from Brazil during the 1970's. I still remember quite well when I was always the first one at the importer's place to see new arrivals. I rushed over as soon as he called me up. Discus by the crate load stood around for sale. Often I had to take my purchase "as is" in their original packaging from abroad. They came packed in plastic bags, eight fish to a bag, in foam cases. Travel time may have lasted as long as thirty-six hours. Hardly any

water filled the bags, in which the fish were upright . . . water was weight, and weight cost a lot of money to ship. It wasn't rare that many of the fish didn't survive the trip. These were reasons for the high price of good specimens.

The newly imported royal blues I bought under those conditions from 1973 to 1977 grew well and took on a very good coloration. I naturally also participated in the risk, since all these discus came directly from the airport. I had hardly any losses, and I attribute that to my conditioning of these fish in a two-meter-

Manaus, Brazil, the center of the discus world. Almost all of the wild-caught discus are shipped from Brazil, primarily by Turkis Aquarium, the firm originated by Willi Schwartz.

miserable-looking discus languishing in the tanks of many shops. Only well managed businesses with a feel for dealing with discus and knowledge of how to keep them can offer quality fish for sale. Each individual hobbyist has to contribute by creating and recognizing standards of quality for discus, and pet shops have to pay more attention to their discus. The dealer's motto should be: "Be attentive to aquarists who breed discus," because caring for homebred fish is definitely a happier chore than dealing with the Asiatic ones.

Germany, for example, has the market and the interest for these charming domestically produced fish. The young fish are easily obtained, even in large quantities, though the adults are available only in limited supply. Many a hobbyist must have made great efforts to purchase quality specimens, only to return home in utter disappointment. Quality breeding pairs that really breed smoothly can't be bought cheaply. What hobbyist wants to sell his own happily

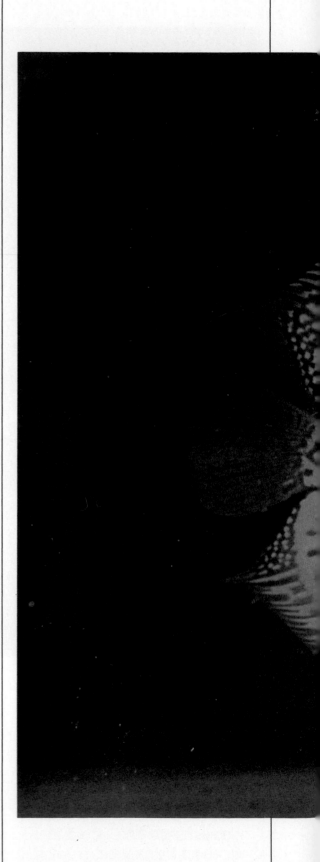

Dr. Clifford Chan photographed these champion discus bred by Mr. Gan Khian Tiong in Singapore. Note the elongations of the dorsal and anal fins, a characteristic of many Thai and Singapore-bred discus.

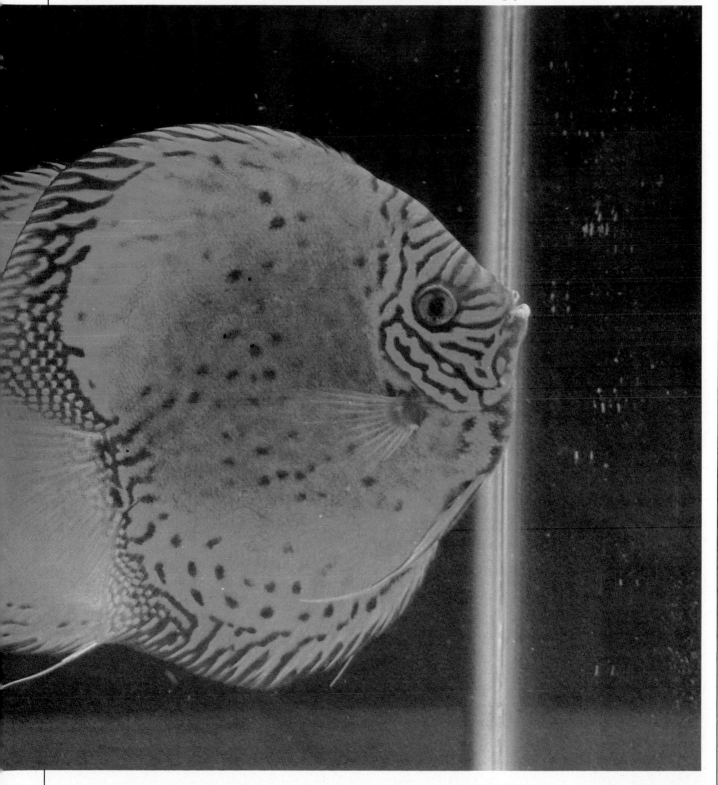

This is not the most desirable of discus breeding setups. The bottoms of the tanks should be clean and not covered with gravel. The tanks could be a little larger, too.

compatible and smoothly living pairs that raise several hundred fry a year for him? There's no need, of course, to answer that question.

I believe that the discus will remain the number one freshwater fish, even in the coming years. Once we've succeeded in maintaining the shape of this species and have dropped the idea that a discus has to be kept only for breeding, we'll have a majestic fish swimming around in our tanks.

Why can't you keep a discus in an exhibition tank along with plants? Well, just try it once with discus. This fish must swim in a bare tank devoid of ground cover and decorated only with a vase. Why can't the discus make its imposing appearance in a natural biotope? When you've read about water plants later in this book, you'll certainly know why I feel the way I do.

The deep tanks in this breeding setup are better than those on the facing page. Actually discus can be spawned in almost any tank large enough to house them and many successful breeders use any tank which is available. The larger the tank the easier it is to control pH, temperature, cleanliness and light.

Discus can be successfully maintained in a heavily planted aquarium, but they would become so shy that you would never see them and more active fish might harass or frighten them.

When the Discus Craze Grabs You

Discus craze, or fever, may well be an apt term, considering that the aquarist who has once kept this fish won't let it go again very fast. This fish, a real housepet, can fascinate its owner. Why this fascination? Well, now, the discus is a splendid fish! It's big and colorful and not nearly as shy as it's often been described. I believe it really recognizes its keeper. The discus can live to a ripe old age, ten to fifteen years easily. And that's yet another reason why the aquarist who deals intensively with discus won't get rid of them quickly.

Perhaps financial considerations also lead an aquarist to start up with discus, for breeding them pays off. Attractively colored young discus quickly fetch buyers at prices that soon begin to convince you to take up this species

A new form Degen is working on has been called 'the Bleeding Heart Discus,' but the author disdains names like that. Note the red splashes on the body. These discus are merely 5 months old and they are already showing modest coloration.

This is a regal Degen discus. This turquoise beauty has the beautiful red eye that Degen tries to achieve in all his varieties.

The brown or red discus, *Symphysodon aequifasciata axelrodi*, with its young feeding from its sides.

wholeheartedly. The discus is the only exception among the exotics or "tropical" fish that—after a reasonable consideration of the real costs involved—can be deemed *financially* worth breeding. You can doubtless sell 100 swordtails for a good price, but the monetary or material outlay to breed 100 swordtails is not much less than that needed to breed 100 young discus. Both species need six to eight weeks before sale. The difference lies in the price. Invariably, the discus fetches at least ten times what the swordtail would bring.

Discus enthusiasts are ready and willing to travel hundreds of miles to buy good discus specimens. As long as they do this, it'll be good for the discus—and it will certainly be good also for the successful discus breeder.

Fifty years ago, angelfish were very difficult to breed. Then, when tank-raised specimens became available, more and more inbred strains were developed. This is a new strain developed in Germany. The fins are very blue and the body is basically silver and gold.

This is a typical, less-expensive type of turquoise discus in which the red stripes are poorly developed. The more colorful the strain, the more valuable it is.

How to Select Discus

Though you may not yet have any discus, the reading of this book may have inspired you to the point of making you run right out to buy some. So you run directly to the closest pet shop to satisfy that impulse. How disappointing not to find any! So you run further to the next shopping center or another part of town, but you still don't find any discus for sale. Maybe they tell you it's not worth their while to sell this fish. They're too expensive or difficult to keep or too sensitive, and so on. Perhaps eventually you find a shop that does sell discus; now there are a few rules to follow. Take your time, a lot of time, when buying fish. What do you really want to buy? Several young ones? A pair of adults? Or perhaps a pair that can breed soon? What kind of coloration would you prefer? That's an important question. Turquoise is most in demand.

Turquoise—solid and striped—discus continue

Turqoise discus are at their best in semi-darkness and with reflected light. Under these conditions most of the reds are lost but the blues become metallic.

Facing page: Longfinned turquoise discus bred by Gan Khian Tiong in Singapore. Photo by Dr. Clifford Chan.

Dr. Schmidt-Focke calls this his red strain. It actually is an enhanced *Symphysodon aequifasciata haraldi.*

to lead the market. The discus for you is a matter of personal preference. A purely solid color has to be intense; if it's not, it becomes monotonous. The coloration of a striped turquoise is always somewhat more refreshingly vibrant. The stripes somehow make it more intriguing. They always have to be thoroughly striped or colored, for when you succeed in breeding them, buyers will always look for what they deem to be excellent in any parents they buy. These demands drive the price of good fish upwards.

Red eyes are important. Specimens with yellow or amber-colored eyes are unfortunately undesirable fish. Red eyes are your trump card. Watch for them when you buy. Note that discus that have been treated with certain drugs lose their red eye color, though it returns when the drug is discontinued or filtered out of the water.

Now let's get on to the actual sale of discus specimens. Important points for buying discus are as follows:

— Note the shape of the fish. It should be as round as possible.

If you must net a discus, use a very fine, soft net. Don't keep the fish out of water too long, especially when picking parasites or applying medicine to the discus' body.

observe it as it swims around the tank. How about the droppings? If you discover white fecal threads several centimeters long in the tank, don't buy these fish; they have intestinal parasites that can be cleared up only with difficulty. Black droppings, on the other hand, are always a good sign. You may be able to see the fish as it releases its droppings, and, if all looks good, buy it if that's the fish you like.

If you want to buy several fish, especially large, fully grown ones, feed them. Don't give too much, but just enough to see if they react to food. A fish's interest in food indicates something of its health. Healthy fish appreciate any handout. Sick fish can hardly be made to eat.

The gills are another point to watch when buying fish. The discus, particularly, is susceptible to gill worms and other parasites. That causes the fish to breathe on only one side. That is, only one operculum can be raised; the other stays closed. Gill worms are bothersome creatures that make life difficult for a discus. This problem

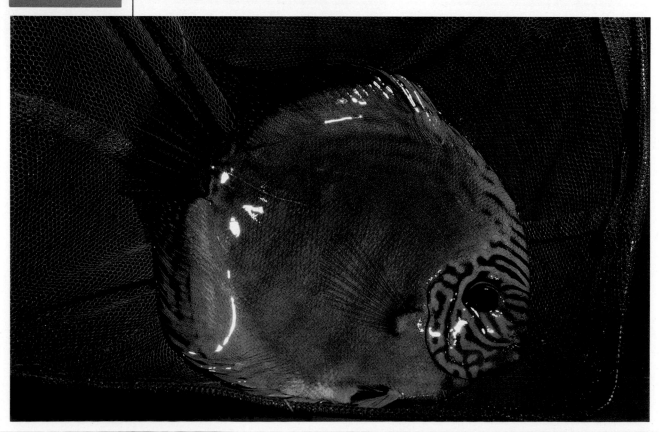

can be resolved with medications, but you've got to spend quite some time taking care of these sick fish. For an experienced discus aquarist, however, a health problem is not necessarily an obstacle to buying a fish, as long as the seller is made aware of the shortcoming.

A discus's coloration also can indicate health status. Frightful looking, darkly colored specimens should be observed closely before they are bought.

If the fish are fed in your presence, you should wait awhile before netting and carrying them away. They could regurgitate or leave their droppings in their travel water "packaging," contaminating it too rapidly.

Use so-called "oxygen tablets" with caution when transporting fish. These tablets, if they involve hydrogen peroxide, may generate too much oxygen, severely irritating the fish and killing it. It's better to transport the fish in a lot of water. Take care, too, when shipping in Styrofoam containers. Use a large bag. Don't ship fish directly in

This is a Japanese-bred turquoise discus. Far Eastern discus breeders rely heavily on German and American breeding stock.

This lovely discus is one stage in the development of the all-blue turquoise envisioned by Jack Wattley many years ago. Wattley has created the most distinctive fish of all the American discus breeders. He is widely respected for his pioneering efforts.

Styrofoam boxes, even though they're watertight, because frightened fish dash wildly around and can seriously injure themselves. If you ship fish in small bags, remember that larger specimens can break through, and use two bags, one inside the other. For valuable specimens, three bags—one inside the others—should not be too much trouble or expense.

It could be catastrophic to pack newspapers in between the bags. If a fish broke through a bag, all its water could be soaked up by the newspaper, leaving the fish to suffocate. A three-ply system (using three bags) prevents that.

When you come home with the fish, take enough time to transfer it *slowly* to its new quarters. Let the temperature of the water you just brought home approach that of your tank. Put some of the tank water into the bag to accustom your new discus to its new tank. If possible, transfer the fish to your tank without pouring in the fish's transportation water. Disease can easily be transmitted by the water from the dealer's tank.

This is an American descendant of a red turquoise strain developed by Degen.

A red turqoise discus developed in America.

If the dealer has an oxygen bottle or tank, you won't have any transportation problems. Pure oxygen released into the bag guarantees problem-free transportation. I've always used oxygen like that when I sold fish. Back in 1974 to 1978, when I used to ship newly captured wild specimens as well as bred specimens by railway express, there were never any problems when a shot of oxygen was included in the bags. Even stretches of 36 hours were no problem for the fish. Temperature, which can gradually drop off, was the main problem. A slowly falling temperature down to about 20°C (70°F) doesn't affect the discus, though the temperature has to be slowly raised again before transferring the fish.

Large discus should always be shipped in bags, but smaller young ones can also be carried in a bucket with a lid. While traveling, the fish like to lie flat on the bottom, which isn't any indication of anything wrong.

Developing a Breeding Line

Every aquarist who has ever kept discus will also try to breed them. We know that it isn't easy to do, but this book is supposed to help you to do it. The prerequisites for a successful breeding program are the selection of good breeding fish and the development of a breeding line.

How do you go about building up a breeding line? The simplest but also the most time-consuming way would be to buy large quantities of youngsters, which you then raise to adulthood. Although a discus can spawn at about one year of age, its active breeding phase usually doesn't begin until it's a year and a half old, so you've got to practice patience.

The advantage of this simple method, though, is the possibility of obtaining offspring of various parents, raising them to adulthood and then appropriately mating them. For this, however,you should

A female blue discus guarding newly-laid eggs.

The Degen red turquoise discus is accepted as one of the most desirable discus varieties bred to date.

The legendary red checkerboard turquoise developed by Dr. Eduard Schmidt-Focke is one of the most expensive of the various discus color varieties.

purchase at least twenty young discus, since you will soon see that these fish grow at different rates and can also sport quite different colorations. I've always sorted out my fish, especially the adolescents. Keep the best of them—judging by their growth and color— and give the rest away. Don't compromise. When discus enthusiasts come to you later or to buy young fish, the sight of a single poor-quality specimen can often turn a prospective buyer away from you. The buyer immediately assumes that this one miserable-looking fish could have something to do with the young fish near it. If you keep only prime specimens, sales should run smoothly.

Unfortunately, the raising of fish fry is not only a time-consuming affair, but it also requires a great deal of patience and effort to turn these discus into good breeding fish. Disease can retard the progress of the young fish, poor growth can result, and still other problems can dampen the joy of raising your own fish. Your discus gobble up food wildly for weeks, then suddenly, from one day to another, it's all over! For no

This female turquoise is normally quite blue, but when the fry feed from her sides, she darkens considerably.

This turquoise male, American bred, discus is in the process of spawning.

apparent reason, feeding suddenly becomes a problem.

If you want to sidestep these problems, buy adult or almost adult discus right from the start. It's not so easy, of course, to find prime adult or yearling specimens, but with some luck and time you can eventually do it. When out shopping around for fish, heed the hints given previously. Yearling turquoise discus are relatively less expensive than older, known breeders. The young ones, though, can theoretically start spawning soon, and that can lead to the most unexplainable things. One breeder can have five genuine pairs that won't spawn, yet a beginner can buy two discus that instantly start spawning the moment he takes them home! I've had all that happen to me at one time or another. Discus breeding also requires a certain measure of luck.

If you've decided to buy adult discus, you should have a clear idea of what coloration you want. Captured wild specimens are scarcely available, at least not with prime coloration, so you've got to rely on breeders. In

Germany, the turquoise discus is absolutely number one. In the German aquarist magazines, the ads for fish are almost all for

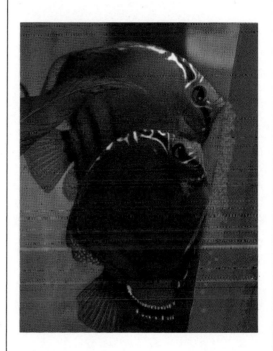

turquoise discus. Other names, though, such as red turquoise, pearl-red turquoise, striped turquoise and solid turquoise can only lead to confusion.

The color of the discus has been subjected to somewhat of a fashion trend. Simple brown ones are simply no longer in demand, though the memory of a brown one captured in the wild still lingers about in the back of my head, for that was the one I started with.

This historical photo was taken by the late Gene Wolfsheimer for the cover of the first edition of Dr. Axelrod's *Encyclopedia of Tropical Fishes*. Taken in the 1950's, it is considered to be the first spawning of *Symphysodon a. axelrodi* and the first disclosure that the fry eat slime from the parents' bodies.

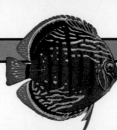

Perhaps the lack of interest in brown is that no one sees brown discus anymore. Maybe many people might like to witness an imposing school of brown, newly captured wild discus if they had the chance. But that wouldn't change a thing. The young would hardly sell.

A second example is the Heckel discus, which no one wants. People are disturbed by the three broad longitudinal stripes that distinguish this discus from the others. This is also the reason why captured wild Heckel discus are sold dirt cheap. Make certain, especially with the Heckel discus, that your prospect has red eyes, since many defective *Symphysodon* have yellow eyes.

Now for a word on the blue and green specimens captured in the wild. Wild blue captives should be completely striped with blue stripes. Then they're sold as royal blue discus. If you come across a well colored wild specimen like that, buy it. Crossing a captured wild discus with a captive-bred one is always an interesting project for a breeder.

Green discus are sold as Tefe discus, which have green stripes on the

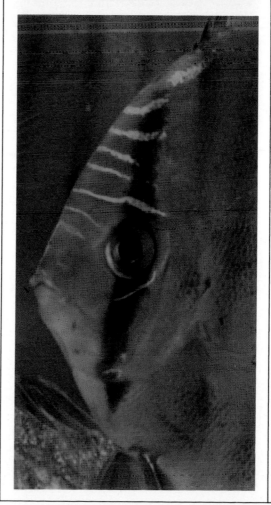

Facing page: A pair of wild brown discus, *Symphysodon a. axelrodi,* spawning.

The faces of a pair of brown or red discus, *Symphysodon aequifasciata axelrodi.* The upper fish, with the more pointed face, is a male. The lower fish, with the more rounded face, is a female. This characteristic is very variable and cannot always be depended upon.

Dr. Herbert R. Axelrod collected this green discus in Lake Tefe, Brazil. It is scientifically known as *Symphysodon aequifasciata aequifasciata*. These were the fish he gave to breeders all around the world and from which it is thought the modern turquoise strains developed. Dr. Axelrod photographed this fish in the wild and later identified it against the type. Note the red eye!

head, back and abdomen. They are, unfortunately, usually not completely striped, but they often show attractive red dots distributed over the body. Specimens with a lot of red can make good crosses.

seasonal flooding of the Amazon and its tributaries. Yet, you still have the beautiful aquarium-bred specimens available. If you're following the vogue, then you'll want turquoise discus with red.

The above-mentioned discus are races captured in the wild; they are becoming harder and harder to find because the costs of fuel and transportation have risen sharply. Also, discus are captured only at certain times of the year. That's easily understood when you consider the

The color red is still the desirable color with discus breeders. Perhaps they're trying to breed a line of vibrantly red discus. The water characteristics, especially its iron content, are of particular importance for that.

The good thing about purchasing an adult

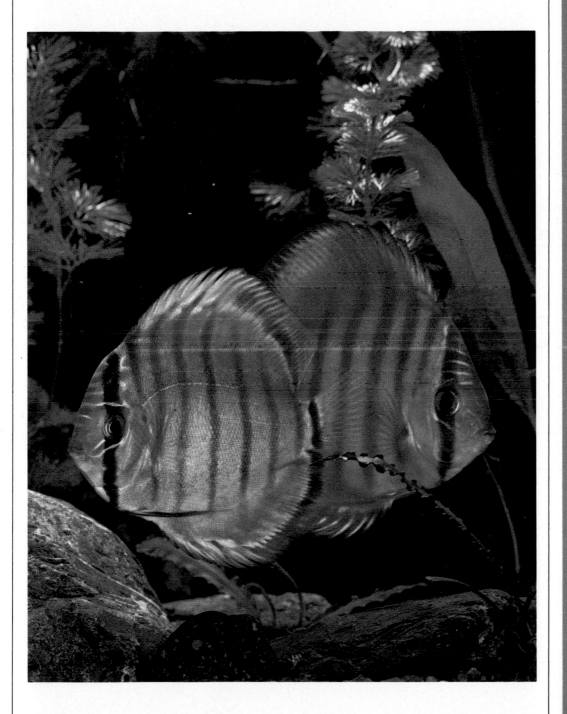

A pair of normal wild brown discus, *Symphysodon aequifasciata axelrodi*. The female has the rounded face, while the male has the more pointed face.

This albino discus created quite a sensation in America, but in Europe and the Far East it was not considered as anything special as all albino fishes are weak and troublesome and none has become 'fashionable.'

discus is that you can readily see its color, shape and fins in their final form. With young fish, however, those points are always somewhat of a risk.

When I visited the U.S.A. I found quite fantastic color designations for discus specimens. There were dotted blue discus, albino discus, cobalt discus, ghost discus and electric blue discus. The Americans prefer

intensive coloration, but most of the discus I saw in the States were of lower quality, which may well be the result of the quite different view taken by American aquarists. Plastic plants, colorful gravel, skulls and divers often are part of an American aquarium. Considering all of that, we can say that German discus are among the best, a view also held by American discus expert Jack Wattley, who travels regularly to Germany to stay in touch with German breeders.

One of the early imports of *Symphysodon aequifasciata haraldi*.

This is a full-
bodied pair of
turquoise
discus with
elongated rays in
the dorsal and
anal fins. These
elongated fins
are characteristic
of Singapore and
Thai discus.

Breeding and Exhibition Tanks

The typical discus tank has no bottom cover, and there are no decorative items whatsoever. This is for a particular reason: to keep the tank clean, which is a prerequisite for breeding. The only other object besides a heater and filter in the tank is a clay or ceramic cone. The fish are supposed to lay their eggs on the cone.

The size of a discus tank is probably debatable, but a capacity of 300 liters (about 75 gallons) is too much and would be uneconomical, since breeding requires a water temperature of 30°C (86°F).

Ideal tanks are 50 cm wide × 50 to 60 cm deep (front to back) and 50 cm high, which means a water content of 125 or 150 liters. That's completely adequate. A great advantage of this tank is that the young discus can school better together and the parents can lead their young

better around the tank. Occasionally a school of new youngsters can't find their parents, so they spread out throughout the whole tank and finally end up dying off. Smaller tanks therefore provide greater chances of success.

If you arrange several breeding tanks next to one another, take care that the adjacent breeding pairs can't see each other. You'd do well to place a sheet of colored paper or board between the tanks to break the line of sight. If the pairs glimpse one

This red turquoise was bred in Singapore. It won Second Prize at the 1989 Singapore Aquarama Show judged by Dr. Herbert R. Axelrod.

The proper size of a discus tank is debatable. A 75 gallon tank is too large . . . maybe a 50 gallon tank?

The beautiful red eye, the hi-fin shape and the intense coloration of this magnificent specimen are the result of selective inbreeding by a Singapore discus breeder.

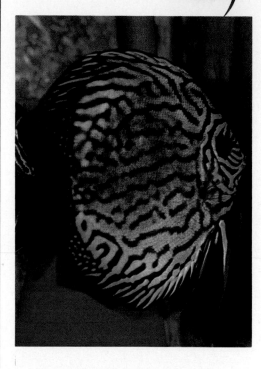

Japanese breeders have produced a more metallic green sheen in their turquoise which they call 'Midori'.

another, they can break out in sham battles at the panes facing each other's territory. The parents are often distracted even from spawning so much that a clutch may be only very poorly fertilized, or even not at all. I once had this situation despite even having cut off their view of one another, except for a small portion of the neighboring tank, which was not cut off from view. The male of the pair constantly held his attack stance, almost completely ignoring his egg-depositing mate; the result was that all the eggs finally were parasitized by fungus.

Since discus can get rather pugnacious even

as adolescents, the number of tank residents has to be correspondingly adjusted. The school always has a dominant fish and a loser, whose growth is stunted. If you remove this weaker fish, another fish will immediately be oppressed in its stead. If you transfer the weaker one to another tank with smaller fish, it will assume the leader's role. Then, if you introduce a larger and stronger specimen into the tank with that formerly weak and subjected but now dominant fish, the new leader will defend its territory and dominate the newly introduced stronger specimen.

Larger tanks can be outfitted with

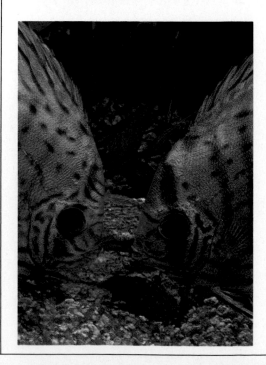

Young discus have a schooling tendency which they begin to lose when they are about 6 months of age, like the fish shown here. It is best to keep discus sorted by size.

correspondingly more effective filters, or connected up to a filtration installation.

It is incontestable that a sterile tank is not only practical to achieve, but is important for breeding. A discus tank embellished with aquatic plants would be far more attractive than a bare, down-to-business tank in which half a dozen frightened discus hover about. But aquatic plants and discus—are they compatible? The only answer to that is, naturally, what could be finer for an aquarist than to have a planted tank plus discus?

Much has been accomplished in recent years in the area of aquatic plants. I remark especially the efforts of the Dennerle brothers, who brought aquatic plants of unique quality into German pet shops. Good German aquatic plant breeding and acclimatized imported plants allow for splendid underwater landscaping. Try it for yourself. There are, however, a few conditions. Aquatic plants need a nourishing substrate, just as in nature, and that not only promotes vegetative growth, but also stabilizes the whole aquatic milieu of the tank. Aquatic plants need a gentle bottom circulation around the roots to supply nutrients. Oxygen, however, shouldn't reach

A discus tank embellished with aquatic plants would be far more attractive than a bare tank.

Most professional breeders opt for a bare tank, bare bottom, lots of space, and but a few fish in each tank. This lovely turquoise Degen discus has proven a hit with the export (from Germany) market.

the roots, because many mineral substances would be oxidized to water-insoluble components. Plants, for example, assimilate only ferrous iron (that is, iron ions with two valences), while the ferric form of iron (with three valences) formed by the oxygen can't be assimilated by the plant. Aquatic plants prefer a uniform, gentle filtration; they don't like to stand in a strong current.

Carbon dioxide (CO_2) has become the magical element in aquatic plant tanks. Complete systems have been developed to provide carbon dioxide to the tanks. There's normally too little carbon dioxide, for the plants very rapidly consume all of it contained in the water. Then there's a carbon dioxide deficiency and the plants suffer. If you could supply additional carbon dioxide, there would be a burst of plant growth. It's really a mistake to think that the addition of fertilizer can correct the deficiency in carbon dioxide. The plants need carbon dioxide even to utilize these fertilizers. Try to keep a carbon dioxide level of 20 to 40 milligrams per liter in the tank. Exactly how much

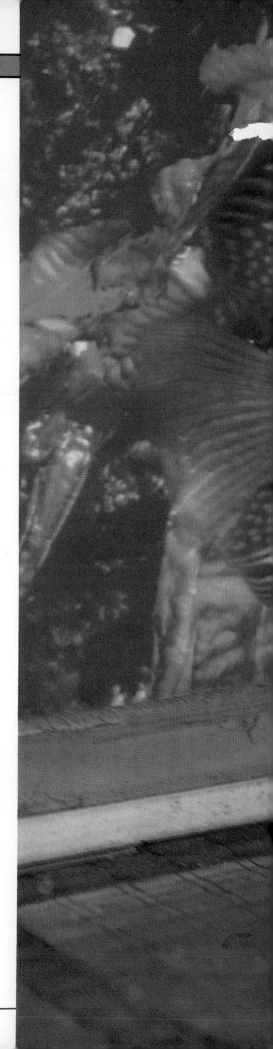

Vallisneria tortissima, oftentimes referred to as 'corkscrew Val', should be planted in bunches to be more effective for the discus tank.

Facing page: This photo, from a Japanese magazine, shows the quality of turquoise fish being bred in Japan in 1989.

carbon dioxide has to be given, however, depends upon several factors, as tabulated below:

High Carbon Dioxide Level Required

Large aquaria
Hard water (carbonates)
Open tanks
Bright lighting
Many plants
Vigorous water movement

Lower Carbon Dioxide Level Required

Small aquaria
Soft water (carbonates)
Covered tanks
Low-intensity lighting
Few plants
Gentle water movement

Don't conclude, however, that low-level lighting makes supplemental carbon dioxide superfluous. A plant can't grow without light. For a nicely arranged discus tank containing 300 liters of water, use between 3 and 6 grams of carbon dioxide daily, adjusted as indicated by the above factors.

High concentrations of carbon dioxide, of course, can be harmful, though

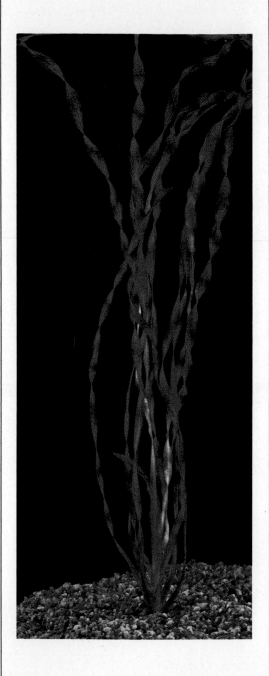

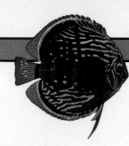

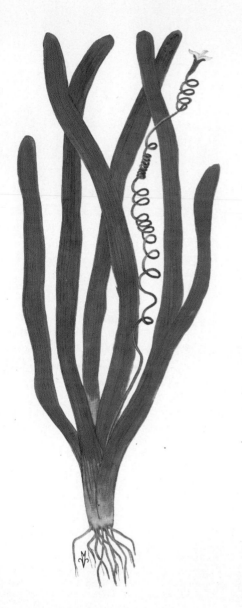

Giant Val, *Vallisneria gigantea,* is ideal for the larger discus tank. It must be planted in stands of about 6 plants in a cluster to be effective.

these levels are not reached in an aquarium. A harmful effect begins to occur above 15 grams per 100 liters of water. Guppies tolerate carbon dioxide concentrations of up to 80 grams per 100 liters of water. Carbon dioxide systems on the market now are tailored to aquarium use and are quite desirable for aquatic plants.

Here are general tips on planting a discus tank. Always plant the same kinds together in groups, unless you're just putting in a single plant for show. Don't mix up all the species in a confused arrangement, but create centers of interest. Don't plant only one *Vallisneria,* but put in five or ten pieces at once. That creates a tranquil background in front of which you can arrange smaller species of plants. In the foreground, a "lawn" or low *Echinodorus* species stands out nicely.

Your work is easier if you lay out a plan for the plantings. Remember that the aquarium needs several weeks before the plants take hold. A freshly planted tank, of course, looks finished, but needs time. Well cleaned bog wood or roots can be

The drawing on the facing page is the same species as the one shown in the photograph except the living plant throws off some shoots which are curly. This is undoubtedly the best plant for the discus tank if the tank gets enough light. 'Enough light' means the plant grows.

Left: Common Val, *Vallisneria americana*, is available at most petshops and does fairly well in the discus tank if it gets enough light.

Right: If the tank does not get enough light, you should try *Cryptocoryne spiralis*, which is a hardy, slow-growing plant which does pretty well in the shade.

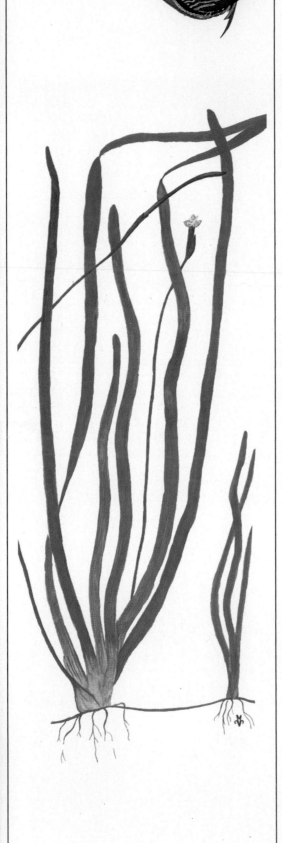

used as decoration and shelter for discus, which like to spawn among these roots, perhaps soon giving you a new discus generation. That's been shown to be effective, though raising youngsters here is more difficult.

Not every aquatic plant is suitable for inclusion in a discus tank, for in a planted discus tank you have a temperature of 27 to 28°C (81 to 83°F). Only a few plants, however, can't tolerate this temperature. Plants that succumb usually do so because of a carbon dioxide deficiency, not because of the heat.

The following plants are particularly suitable for discus tanks:

Aponogeton crispus does very well in the discus aquarium, but it requires light. Sometimes a small spotlight can highlight the plant and supply its lighting needs.

Cryptocoryne beckettii is easy to cultivate, but it too needs light to thrive.

Echinodorus argentinensis is a very sturdy-leafed plant. Often the discus will spawn on the plant leaf.

Aponogeton crispus (Ruffled sword plant or water ear)

A. rigidifolius (Stiff-leaved water ear)

A. ulvaceus (Madagascan ulva-leaved water ear)

A. undulatus (Thai wavy water ear)

Bolbitis heudelotii (Congo aquatic fern)

All *Cryptocoryne* species on the market

All *Echinodorus* species, which usually come from Amazonia.

Microsorium pteropus (Java fern, previous *Gymnopteris)* and all *Vallisneria* species.

Microsorium pteropus is a lovely plant which does well if its light requirements are met.

Left:
*Aponogeton
ulvaceus.*
Below:
*Cryptocoryne
beckettii .*

Cryptocoryne affinis does well in subdued light. It has a lovely reddish underside.

Echinodorus maior grows well in a discus aquarium because the discus do not chew on its delicate leaves.

Technical Layout

SAFE HEATING FOR AQUARIA

Safety is concern number one in aquaristics, too. Heating is of great concern here because we're dealing with the direct immersion into water of a source of electrical current. Electricity in water naturally always implies danger. So tank heating has to be as safe as possible. What kind of heating system is good to use? In my opinion, the rod-shaped thermostatically regulated submergible heater leads the others. It's simply irreplaceable. I've been using a good brand of adjustable heaters for over fifteen years; they can be closely regulated.

I was naturally interested in what would happen if a heater were damaged in the tank. Let's assume for a moment that fish knock your heater against the wall of the tank and break the instrument open. Well, nothing happens to the fish. Some current leakage around the heater would make the fish uncomfortable, and they'd simply swim away from the heater. If the hobbyist reached into the water, however, he'd soon notice it. He'd get a little tickling shock if he dipped in far from the broken heater, but a real jolt if he were closer to it. If he were grounded, then the electricity, under certain circumstances, would pass through his body.

The intensity of the electrical current would at least partly depend upon the conductivity of the

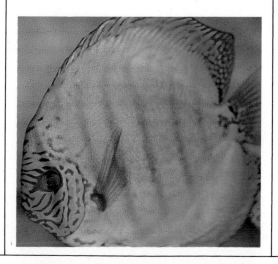

A Singapore-bred turquoise.

A Singapore-bred turquoise.

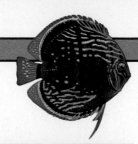

This magnificent discus was bred in Singapore and won a prize at the 1989 Aquarama.

water. Since there's only a low level of mineral salts in a discus tank, the water is a poorer conductor than the water in a marine tank—but it's still dangerous. The first rule of operating in an aquarium should therefore be: First disconnect the heater from the electrical source! Receptacles and plugs with on and off switches make it easy to break the circuit merely by pushing a button or throwing a switch.

FILTRATION SYSTEMS

There are innumerable aquarium filters, but not all of them are suitable for discus tanks, especially a breeding tank. Discus like calm, almost still, water and dislike constantly having to swim against a

A Singapore-bred turquoise.

filtration current, especially in a tank 50 to 60 cm long. A breeding tank must be calm, and that includes the filtration system, too.

Since discus prefer acidic water with a pH of 6 on the average, it could be useful to use peat for a filtration medium if possible, thus regulating the pH value. Filtration, in any case, must be done. So we have to decide only which system seems most appropriate. Let's examine the breeding tank first. The filter shouldn't be too large for a tank of 125 to 150 liters capacity. If you breed discus, you'll certainly not limit yourself to only one tank, but two or three tanks lined up adjacent to one another. These tanks are best serviced by compact internal filters, each of which purifies its

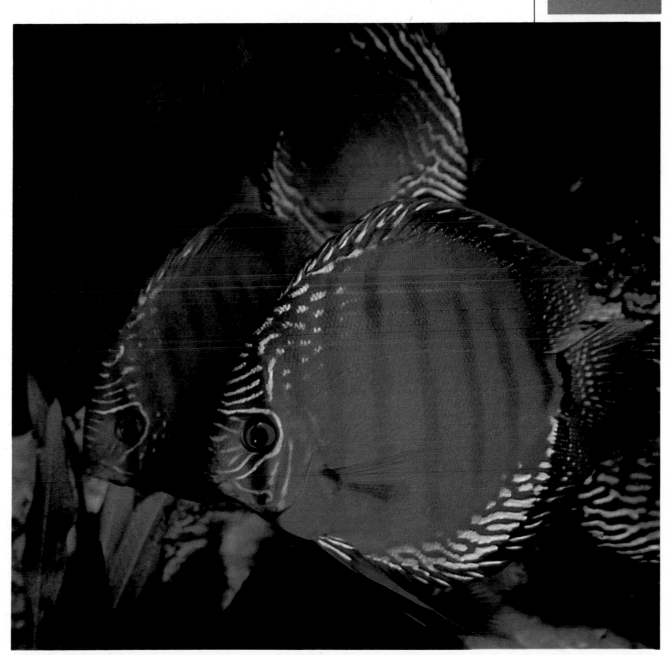

This lovely German brown or red discus, *Symphysodon aequifasciata axelrodi*, is considered the most difficult subspecies to breed.

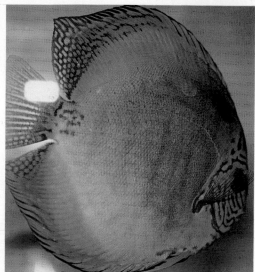

A nice light turquoise from Thailand.

A red turquoise from Singapore breeders.

own tank. This independence prevents the transmission of disease among the tanks.

What type of filtration should you use in a discus breeding tank? Well, first you've got two fish in the tank, but they don't dirty it up very much. If you vacuum off the largest pieces every three days with a bottom vacuum device, or replace 20 liters of water, the filter can take care of all the rest. When the discus spawn, it takes about six days after the spawning until the fry start swimming. During those six days, you can't change too much water, so the filter has to clean up alone. Once the young discus are free-swimming, you have to throttle down the filter for fourteen days to avoid vacuuming up the youngsters. But then you can start vacuuming up again, because the young will be swimming close to their parents and won't come near your vacuum device. After these fourteen days, you can turn up the filter again, since the little ones won't run the risk of being "filtered out" any more.

After consideration of all of this, you'll realize that an internal filter with foam

filler and which permits long-term operation is the most suitable.

I bought two different models of such filters in an effort to discover which was best for the breeding tank. The smaller of the two at first seemed too weak to me for a 125-liter (about 30 gallons), but I still tried it. In practice, the small filter quickly proved to be just what the doctor ordered for a tank of this size. I tried out the larger filter in a 250-liter tank that housed six adolescent discus, and this filter was able to filter out all the filth these "teenagers" produced; I naturally also siphon up a bit once or twice a week and replace a portion of the water.

The most fascinating thing about these two filters is that the small filter consumes only three watts and the large one only 10 watts per hour. Those are figures, of course, that make multiple use of filters of this kind very interesting economically.

Large tanks work well with a large external filter. A rectangular glass tank is used as a filter box. This outside filter should be as large as possible. The most appropriate would be to connect a series of

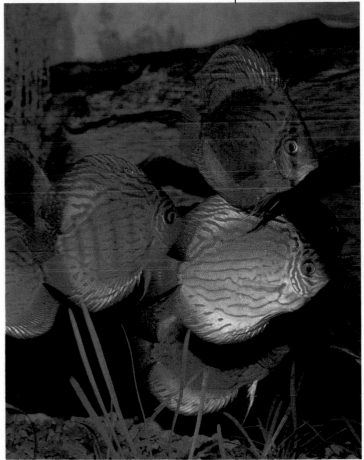

These are really beautiful German turquoise with nice red eyes.

These are nicely growing youngsters with their wild *Symphysodon aequifasciata haraldi* parents.

A tank-raised *Symphysodon aequifasciata axelrodi* shown in Singapore in 1989.

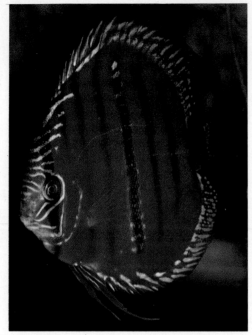

A Singapore-bred turquoise discus.

tanks via piping, which would look like, for example, three tanks next to one another in a single installation, making a filtration reservoir which shows at least 10% or, better, 20% of the tank water to be filtered. Tanks not being used anymore, of course, are very good for this. Glue in partitions to make one or two chambers in the tanks, so that you have a pre-filtration chamber with a sieve and filter floss, then a gravel or other crushed stone chamber, and then finally a clear water chamber. The pre-filtration chamber receives the water collected from the tank via the pipes. The sieve

you hang inside (a large kitchen colander) with some floss catches the largest particles of debris.

The sieve can then easily be cleaned weekly. In the first, floss-filled chamber and in the gravel chamber, the water is filtered and undergoes biological degradation by the resident bacteria. In the clear-water chamber, the purified water is pumped by means of an efficient submerged pump back to the tanks via the pipes, thus completing the filtration cycle.

Underwater oil-cooled rotary pumps can include a complete plumbing system with all connectors and valves for

These 6 month old German turquoise discus are good examples of the quality of discus being raised in Germany in 1989. The photo, taken with available light, shows the metallic sheen of the turquoise to its best advantage.

The four discus shown on this page and the facing page were exhibited at the 1989 Aquarama Show held in Singapore. These, and the other photos of discus on exhibit and shown on other pages in this book, are representative examples of the varieties of discus being produced in southeast Asia.

regulating water circulation. The advantage of such a system is being able to connect an ozone generator to the clear-water chamber, thus permitting sterilization of the water flowing into the tank. I'd prefer addition of ozone to use of an ultraviolet lamp, since with the ozone device I could accurately measure off the exact dosage, while the performance of an ultraviolet lamp can soon fall off.

BIOLOGICAL FILTER SYSTEMS

Biological filtration systems are constantly being introduced on the market, though small filters with foam cartridges continue to be used for breeding tanks. The important thing with all filters is that the filter medium—gravel, polyester floss, charcoal, etc.—not be completely washed out and cleaned when the filtration system is cleaned. This also applies to the cleaning of the foam filtration cartridges for small inside filters. Repeated complete rinsing still leaves a basic supply of bacteria, though the rinse water shouldn't be too hot.

Both of the large outside filters need only a semi-annual cleaning of the filtration chambers, if the pre-filtration chamber is equipped with a sieve.

OZONIZATION OF TANK WATER

The word *ozone* is unknown to many aquarists who never had any dealings with the problem of ozonization. Aquarists with a community tank probably won't be interested in so much technology. Marine aquarists, on the other hand, have quite another attitude. They ozonize their tanks to improve protein skimming. Ozone has the property of coagulating protein; that is, it does something like "clotting" it, allowing the larger protein particles to be better filtered out. Decomposing proteinaceous matter produces harmful toxins.

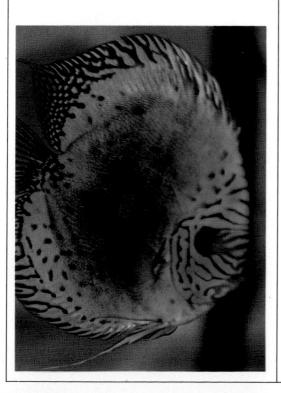

Nitrate is a nitrogenous compound produced by the breakdown of organic matter. Food residues, urine and excretion burden the water. Nitrate develops particularly in aquaria whose filtration systems are too small and which are also overpopulated. If you could supplementally ozonize a tank that possesses an adequate filter in which biological degradation processes could occur, you could then easily lower the nitrate concentration to its ideal level of under 0.1 milligram per liter of water.

Since ozone can prevent an outbreak of disease and heal ectoparasitic diseases, you could perhaps obtain excellent results by ozonizing your discus tank. With ozone,

Asians produce physically different discus with elongated fins and tall bodies, while European and American breeders seem to prefer more intense coloration.

Examples, on these two pages, of the kinds of turquoise varieties produced primarily in Singapore and Thailand.

however, don't administer any (other) medication at the same time.

It's important for us discus enthusiasts to realize that ozone can affect and destroy the discus's skin secretion. That's why tanks containing parents with their young shouldn't be ozonized until that stage is over.

Water Chemistry

Three quality factors— pH, hardness, conductivity—play an important role in discus breeding. Problems arise that the average aquarist doesn't usually encounter or have to deal with in the care and breeding of simple fish. In those cases, simple

assessments with test results is all that's needed. With discus breeding, however, that's not enough. We need accurate measurements, because accuracy is critical for breeding.

Let's start with the pH of the water. "Normal" tap water has a pH value of 7.0 to 8.0.

The pH scale ranges from 0.0 to 14.0, which is a measurement involving the hydrogen ion concentration. Water with a pH value of 7.0 is neutral. If the pH drops, then the water becomes more acidic. If the pH rises, the water becomes more basic or alkaline. Our discus feel most comfortable in a slightly acidic water, that is, a pH just under 7.0. Ideal pH levels are around 6.0, which can be easily achieved by adding peat.

Since this pH level is important for the behavior, appetite and reproduction of our discus, it should be checked regularly. That's why discus breeders soon acquire an electrical pH measuring device to accurately monitor pH. The device's probe or electrode is dipped into the tank water; an electrical current is then amplified and translated into a pH value readable on the device. The pH can be determined accurately within seconds. The electrode can be left submerged in the tank water to provide continued monitoring of the pH; you only have to press a button to read the exact pH at any given moment.

The water's conductivity is another important consideration. All water contains dissolved minerals or salts as ions, which conduct current through the water. The higher the ion concentration, the better the conductivity. Conductivity is very slight in the waters of the natural habitat of the discus; values under 50 microSiemens have been recorded there, which implies a water hardness of 1° DH and less—that is, as good as no carbonate hardness to the water. That has to be the ideal, too, when breeding. Discus will spawn in the hardest of waters, but the osmotic pressure generated by the higher content of minerals destroys the eggs or results in their rapidly being attacked by

pH, hardness and conductivity play an important role in discus breeding.

Toxicity of several metals to fishes

Element	TL_m* (mg/L)**	Probable Safe Concentration (mg/L)**	Extenuations
Aluminum	0.3 (24 hr)	≤ 0.1	Maximum solubility 0.05 mg/L: at pH 7, at least 5 mg/L at pH 9
Antimony	12 to 20 (96 hr)	—	Antimony potassium tartrate toxicity to fathead minnow
Arsenic as arsenite	1.1 to 2.2 (48 hr) 14.1 to 14.4 (29 da)	≤ 0.7 —	May be concentrated in aquatic food chain as an additional source under natural conditions
Cadmium	0.01 to 10.0	≤ 0.001	Related to water hardness, environmental factors, fish species and others
Chromium	5.0 to 118.0 (96 hr)	≤ 0.05	Related to water quality; depends on valence (hexavalent or trivalent chromium) and chemical species
Copper	3.0 to 7.0 (48 hr)	≤ 0.015	Related to water hardness, synergisms and antagonisms of other substances in the water and fish species
Iron	0.1 to 10.0 (24 to 48 hr)	≤ 0.03	Solubility of iron is related to pH; iron hydroxides precipitate onto gills and suffocate fishes at pH 7 or higer; toxicity is related to hardness
Lead	1.0 to 7.0 in soft water, 400+ in hard water (96 hr)	≤ 0.03	Solubility of lead related to pH; toxicity related to water hardness
Manganese	2.2 to 4.1 (24 hr)	—	Permanganates are much more toxic than other manganese species; manganese compounds are unstable and precipitate as manganese oxides or hydroxides at pH above 7.5
Mercury	1.0	average total mercury 0.0005	Biological accumulation 0.5 mcg Hg per g of wet weight aquatic organism
Nickel	5 to 43 (96 hr)	≤ 0.03	Toxicity is related to water hardness

Silver
  as sulfide +
  thiosulfate
  complex
	0.004 to 0.2
	280 to 360
	(96 hr)
		0.0001 to 0.0005
		16 to 35
			Toxicity is related to organic loading of the water, silver, species and other factors

Uranium	2.8 to 135.0 (96 hr)	—	Toxicity is related to water hardness
Zinc	0.87 to 33.0 (96 hr)	≤ 0.05	Toxicity is related to water hardness and to synergism or antagonism of other substances in the water

*TL_m is the "median tolerance limit," where 50% of individuals survive a specified toxicant level for a specified time period.

**mg/L is equivalent to mg/kg, since one liter of water weighs one kilogram.

Heavy metals are the silent killers of the aquarium. While copper test kits are readily available at petshops, tests for iron, zinc, mercury and lead might require a professional laboratory. Since many aquarium fish foods contain large amounts of heavy metals and there are no governmental guidelines specifically for aquarium fish foods, heavy metals should be considered as a factor in mysterious fish deaths.
This chart is provided by Dr. George Post from his wonderful *Textbook of Fish Health* which is available from most pet shops.

fungus. Water in the breeding tank, in any case, should measure less than 300 microSiemens, whereby the carbonate hardness will account for the smaller part of the water hardness. This water would have a hardness of 6° DH.

Since many discus aquarists have very hard tap water, which is unsuitable for use in a breeding tank, they have to demineralize their water.

Ion exchange is the way to go to obtain problem-free mineralized water for discus tanks. Demineralization, however, is usually necessary only when breeding. Harder water can be used in the discus's regular exhibition tank. They can be kept in

hard water with no problem. Since our declared goal, however, is breeding, we have to get involved with demineralization of the water once our tap water goes over 6° DH. It should be obvious that fish do better anyway in water that is subjected to slight fluctuations. Fish that always swim around in the same water of a closed, germ-poor system take a turn for the worse much quicker when their water deteriorates or when they travel or are transferred about.

Fish that live in water with constantly varying chemistry are definitely more stable. Naturally, the fluctuations shouldn't be too large, yet it's quite all right for water that's just been changed to

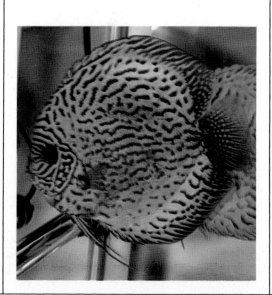

Singapore-bred turquoise discus.

Thai-bred turquoise discus.

The discus shown on these two pages are further examples of fishes produced in Thailand and Singapore and which were on display at the 1989 Aquarium Fish Competition in Singapore.

Ion exchangers may be useful in removing toxic heavy metals from the aquarium water. Activated charcoal may also be useful, but constant water changing is the best.

have a different pH or be harder than usual. Fluctuation of 0.5 pH, for example, is inconsequential when transferring the fish. Of course, transfer of fish always requires a feel for the procedure. Whoever just dumps newly purchased fish right from the plastic carrying bag into the tank can be in for bad surprises. A slow transition is necessary. In that way, these fish can even tolerate a 10° DH difference in water hardness easily.

Cation and anion exchanges are varied. Demineralizers are advertised in the aquaristic publications. The size you need

depends upon the water hardness. You can test the efficacy of the demineralization unit by using a conductometer. Ion exchange proceeds very simply. The water passes over the exchange resin, where the ions are deposited on the resin. If the resin becomes saturated with ions, the exchanger drops in efficiency and the resin has to be regenerated. For that, hydrochloric acid or sulfuric acid is used, according to the manufacturer's instructions.

The anion exchangers Lewatit M600 and M600G3 with color indicator, for example,

are strongly basic resins which also remove nitrates, which is why they are often combined with an acidic resin exchanger. The water runs first through the column with the acidic resin, then through the second column with the strongly basic resin, thus reducing conductivity to practically zero. The pH, however, settles at about 7.0.

At a conductivity of 10° DH for tap water, a liter of resin suffices for demineralizing 200 to 400 liters of water. Depending upon the kind of resin, you can de-carbonize, partially demineralize, completely demineralize, or remove nitrites and humic acids.

The acidic-reacting resins are regenerated with 6% hydrochloric acid. The basic or alkaline anion exchange resins are regenerated with 4% sodium hydroxide. Two liters of regeneration liquid are used for one liter of resin. Complete instructions and recommendations are available from the manufacturers of these products.

With exchange resins, the discus breeder has full control of the water and need not fear any problem from this quarter when breeding his discus.

Fluctuations of 0.5pH are inconsequential when transferring fish from one environment to another.

A prime example of the quality of discus that appeal to European hobbyists. The fish should be intensely colored, stocky, and have nice red in the eye and a balanced series of lines on the body.

Preparations for Breeding

Every discus breeding session starts with the question: "Where can I get a good breeding pair?" That's not an easy question to answer. There are several possibilities. As already described in the chapter on developing a breeding line, you can raise your own adults, which takes time. If you purchase adult or almost adult specimens, you've naturally got to attempt to sex the fish. It's always very difficult to determine the sex of an adult discus. The greatest degree of certainty is afforded only by comparing "littermates" or "nestmates" of the same age. The fins may offer some indication. A comparison may show more of a pointed fin contour, while the female presumably has somewhat rounded off dorsal and ventral fins.

More massive skulls and fat lips and throat sacs are favorite distinguishing features of the discus male—but all that can be misleading. A year or so ago I bought four adult discus that had hatched from the same spawning. Two of them soon paired off for spawning. Left alone in a tank to themselves, they quickly began their spawning preparations. One discus was more

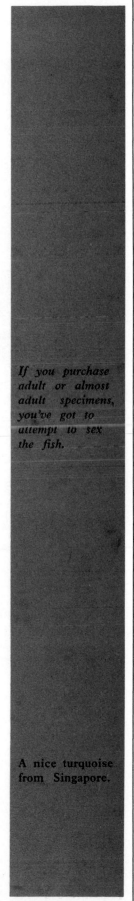

If you purchase adult or almost adult specimens, you've got to attempt to sex the fish.

A nice turquoise from Singapore.

The fishes shown on these two pages were entered into competition at the Aquarama Competition held in Singapore in 1989. They were all bred in southeast Asia from stocks originally acquired in Germany and America.

robust looking; it was about a centimeter larger and seemed to be a typical discus male.

I just happened to be there to observe the whole spawning process. The male turned out to be the female, and, of course, vice versa. I would have lost all bets. This female was large and robust. Unfortunately, she turned out to be an egg eater, so that made her continued use as a breeder questionable.

After she gobbled up the eggs a day after laying them both of the first two times, I hit upon the following way of trying to control that: I fished her out after she laid the eggs. The male then cared for them, but he, too, ate them up. After the next spawning, I

switched around, and took *him* out, but then she again resorted to eating the eggs. Since this pair regularly spawned every week right on the dot, I was able to experiment further. I again removed the male, because the female was quite quarrelsome. I covered the eggs with a perforated Plexiglas beaker and left them to their fate.

She guarded the clutch of eggs as if nothing were different. Fungus covered some of the eggs because they hadn't been fanned, but about half hatched. At that point, I removed the plastic cone, and soon afterwards the female ate up her young.

This pair spawned at least twenty times before they stopped eating up their eggs. Their fighting

grew more and more violent, and one day the raging discus female injured her mate so badly that he died of internal injuries. Unfortunately, I couldn't prevent it.

Then I put a Tefe discus captured in the wild, and of about the same size, into the tank with this raging bride. They both hit it off from the start, and soon they began spawning and produced a large clutch. The fish didn't eat the eggs, but the eggs fungused anyway.

The fungusing should have been impossible with my ideal water chemistry! I live in the country and use my own spring in the garden, whose water is 1°DH, 30 microSiemens and pH 6.5 from the tap. What could I do? Reduce

filtration during spawning so that the milt doesn't wash away? Add methylene blue or malachite green to combat bacterial infection? The next clutch was no better. The virility of the male from the wild was in question. Could they be two females? Everything was possible. I lay in ambush until I could watch them spawning, but those two kept on outsmarting me. Another fungused clutch. That happened several more times.

Then suddenly, a few eggs among the fungused ones appeared to be fertilized. My joy was premature. But no— one single fry hatched

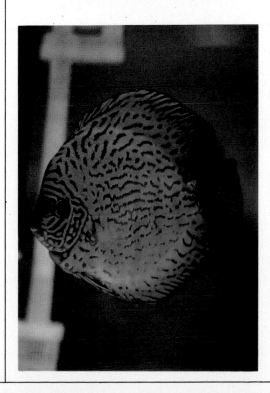

I put a Tefe discus captured in the wild in with a widow, they hit it off, and produced a large clutch of eggs.

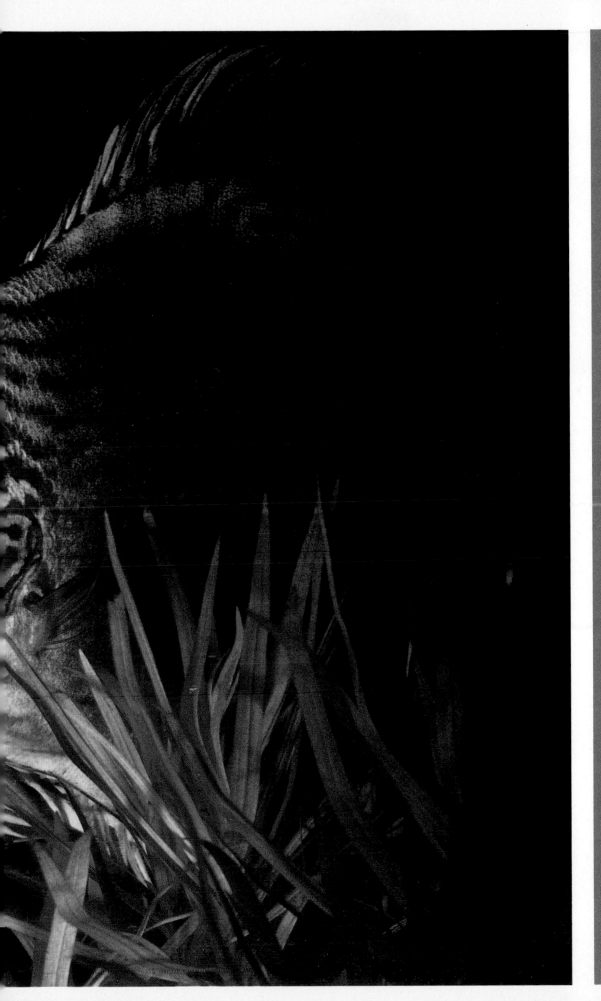

Will wonders
never cease?
This magnificent
pair of discus
spawned right
on top of the
algae on a piece
of driftwood.

Four examples of discus bred in southeast Asia and entered into the Aquarama Competition held in Singapore in 1989. The competition is held every two years. It features very rare fishes, lectures by eminent authorities and commercial displays of aquarium manufacturers.

from a huge bed of fungus. My discus male was really a male! Both parents cared for, with touching attention, their sole heir. After two days' time, however, it disappeared while still in the larval stage. What was important, though, was that I had a real breeding pair and that their egg-eating was over.

I was able to observe them again while spawning. I sat for an hour in front of the tank and learned why the eggs had gone bad. The male fertilized poorly. Only once or twice during spawning did he swim uninterestedly over the eggs, while the female spawned in an exemplary fashion. The result was that I replaced him, too, for I was determined to have this female produce

young, cost what it may.

Since then, she's spawned about thirty times within eight months with the sure-fire brilliant turquoise male I had matched her up with. The replaced mate went to a solid turquoise female in another tank.

These transfers, however, were not very rewarding. The original discus female chased the turquoise male from one corner to the other. She would have dangerously threatened him too, had I not removed him on the second day. That newly introduced male from the wild was not violent, to be sure, but didn't look at his new love even a little bit. So there wasn't anything left for me to do but to reunite them.

The female spawns almost every week, and the eggs no longer get

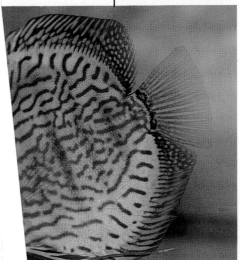

...ken, ...he ...body.

...the ...s ...erior

...s ...The

...gin ...eir ...he

...spawning cone, going at it full force. This vigorous cleansing shows that spawning is imminent. The female's ovipositor is now visible. This broad tube is about three or four millimeters long, so it can be seen. The male's copulatory organ is shorter and slightly pointed. Soon the female makes a dry run

before laying her eggs. She swims upwards along the spawning cone. Now, hopefully, the male won't be distracted any more and stands by, because after a few runs—which can last an hour—the female begins to lay her eggs. She swims up along the spawning cone and lays her eggs in a row. Now would be a favorable moment for the male to swim right behind her and fertilize these eggs. The female goes faster and faster, laying row after row of eggs. Average clutches range from 150 to 200 eggs. "High performance" clutches can go as high as 500 eggs.

A spawning run lasts about an hour. If you're watching the process, you'll get a good idea of harmonious living. The sex of the spawning fish can be determined—a useful characteristic for subsequent pairings.

After the eggs are laid, the parents position themselves in front of the clutch and fan it with their pectoral fins. Harmonious pairs take turns. You can feed them during this phase, but not too much or the food remnants can contaminate the water. The parents don't eat as much now as at other times, anyway. Still, it would certainly be wrong to leave them without *any* food during this whole breeding phase; they need some food.

Good discus eggs are clear. The fry hatch in about sixty hours. This time can be shortened if

the water is 30 to 32°C (86°to 90°F). The ideal temperature is 29 to 31°C (84° to 88°F). The wriggling fry begin to swim free after another 50 to 60 hours.

When the larvae hatch, the parents suck them up and usually transfer them to a spot next to the clutch, where they hang suspended by a thread. Fry that swim free too soon are collected by the parents. It looks as if the parents swallow these precocious young, but once they swim up to the main brood they spit out these runaways among their brood-mates.

As soon as the young swim free, it's important that they swim up to the

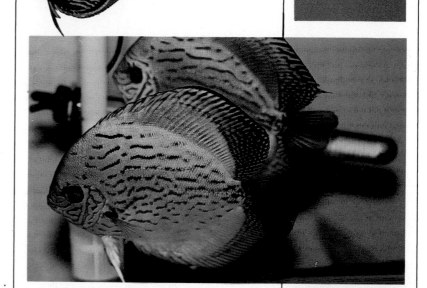

parents, for only in that way will breeding be successful. If they don't find the parents' skin secretion and swim aimlessly around in the tank, they soon die.

For the first four to five days, the fry need only the parental skin secretion to feed on. After that, they're fed hatched brine shrimp nauplii. Soon, in about another fourteen days, you can fall back on supplemental feeding; I use tablets. Keep on feeding *Artemia*, too, for a while longer. This will bring the fry to the size of a quarter in about four weeks. At that point, they can separate from their parents. In a total of six weeks they will have reached a size at which they can be sold.

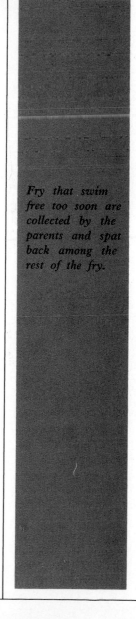

Fry that swim free too soon are collected by the parents and spat back among the rest of the fry.

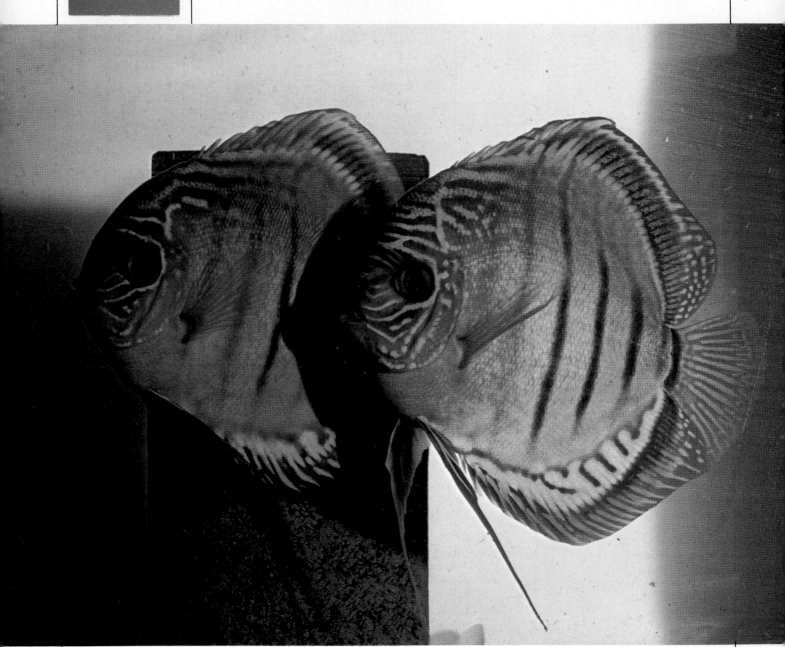

Spawning sites for discus are many and varied. While European discus breeders prefer pottery, American breeders are successful using bricks. As long as the fish accept them, and the spawning sites are easily cleaned, it doesn't matter which type of spawning site you choose.

HELPFUL TRICKS AND SECRETS

This chapter covers useful tips—gathered from actual experience—that can make discus breeding a successful venture for you.

Take a good look at the breeding tank. The ideal standing level at which a discus breeding tank should be situated off the floor is about three inches more than a yard, measured from the bottom edge of the tank. That makes the upper edge of the tank (say a 50-cm high one) 1.50 meters up off the floor. My breeding tank is still another 30 cm higher. Experience shows that the fish at this height don't take fright so easily, perhaps because of the incidental light angle. Discus kept in a leg-high tank are always significantly more skittish—and a discus that takes fright naturally doesn't think of mating.

Fish often become so frightened in a sterile tank devoid of decorative items that they dart about and smash into the sides of the tank. They can even kill themselves like that. Fish from the age of three months on can be seen doing that. The discus recognizes its keeper and is used to his or her calm movements around the tank. If strangers approach the tank, however, their

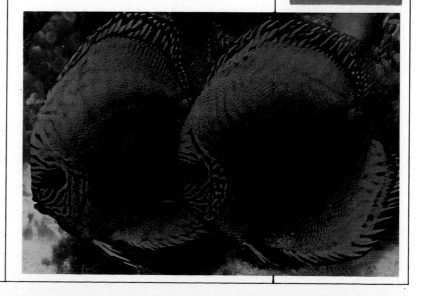

A magnificent pair of dark blue turquoise bred by Gan Khian Tiong, Gan Aquarium Fish Farm in Singapore.

Gan Aquarium Fish Farm giant discus. The intense coloration is a product of good breeding and photography by Dr. Clifford Chan using available light instead of strobe.

approach must be calm and quiet. That's rule number one. Healthy fish that go for their food come up to the front glass out of curiosity to view any visitors who approach. They'll eat right out of your hand at feeding time.

Light, too, plays a role. Since there are no plants in the breeding tank, the illumination can be somewhat weaker than required for a planted tank. Select a warm fluorescent tube. While the breeding pair is still caring for its brood or before spawning, let a small light burn overnight. Hook up a small 15-watt bulb over the tank; that will be adequate. Discus sleep regularly. When you switch on the light in the morning, you'll see that the fish are quietly resting at the bottom. If you tried to feed them immediately then, they'd take nothing. Only after a short wait do the fish become active and then greedily go after their breakfast.

When the fish start spawning and you see it, turn the filter off, but don't keep it off for longer than an hour, of course. Strong currents hinder the fish during spawning and, despite opinions to the contrary, can keep the eggs from being properly fertilized. In the wild, the discus spawn in standing waters.

Since many breeders have to deal with moldy eggs, and since the antifungal agents they use to remedy that problem affect the nutrient mucus secreted by the parents' skin, I've come up with the following method: after

spawning occurs, I add a large amount of methylene blue or malachite green to the water. Pet shops sell solutions of both dyes, and they come with instructions for solution strength and dosage. Both chemicals penetrate human skin, so caution is advised in handling them. As soon as the young hatch, you have to filter out these medications, since they destroy the skin secretion. Jack Wattley uses only methylene blue in breeding, and at very high doses.

Since these medications break down anyway after a few days, the risk of destroying the skin secretion is not great. I've always filtered out the drugs in a few hours with a charcoal charge in the filter just when the eggs hatch. In that way nothing can happen to the mucus, which is slowly developing. This method has proved to work quite well. Once hatching starts, about two days after the eggs are laid, don't use any ozone, since it destroys the skin secretion.

The parents, in some cases, can't secrete any mucus, and then the brood is hopelessly lost. In Germany, a virility-increasing drug in human medicine can help—yohimbin. I've used this drug, and it was effective in helping the parents' mucus production, and I didn't see any harm caused to the fish. An acquaintance of mine believed that the fish

The Singaporeans gave this kind of the discus the name 'leopard discus.' Such names should be discouraged as they are merely for commercial purposes.

Below: A new strain of Gan discus.

One of the unsung discus heroes was Osvaldo Gonzalez who photographed these fish in 1979! The male is a hi-fin turquoise. The female is a cross between a normal brown *Symphysodon aequifasciata axelrodi* and a blue. Fish like these became the basis of the varieties available today.

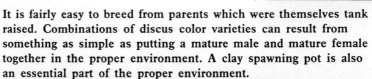

wouldn't spawn again for a long time after having been medicated. But when you've lost several broods because of deficient skin secretion, you might want to try this method.

Another important item in breeding is the spawning pot, usually a conical clay vase at least 20 cm (about 8 inches) high, better 25 cm. Each cone has one bulge or ledge at the bottom and another further up. I developed these conical vases and had them fired because I became aware that wriggling young fish slowly sink and could disappear down into the bottom were the bulging ledge not there to stop them. Every fry lost like that is a bitter loss. The falling fish are caught by the two troughs and stay there until the parents discover and rescue them.

If one of these clay vases wobbles, or if the base is not very smooth, you can apply a silicone cement glue to fill in any irregularities in the rim along the base of the vase. Then stand the cone on a sheet of newspaper, which can be removed with water after the glue dries. The base is now soft and elastic.

It is fairly easy to breed from parents which were themselves tank raised. Combinations of discus color varieties can result from something as simple as putting a mature male and mature female together in the proper environment. A clay spawning pot is also an essential part of the proper environment.

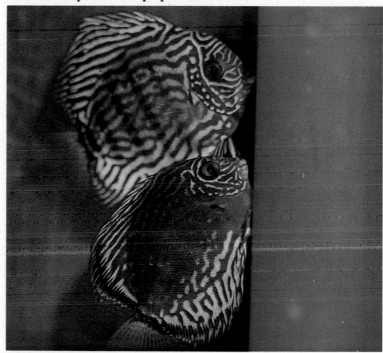

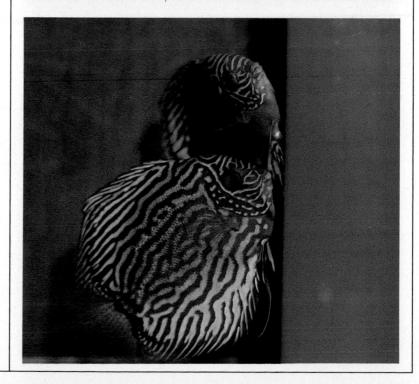

This female *Symphysodon aequifasciata haraldi* is laying her eggs on a flowerpot while the male turquoise anxiously awaits his chance to fertilize the newly laid eggs.

Other means of accelerating the breeding of discus include raising the temperature by 2°C (about 3.5°F) and an extensive change of water, whereby the new water has a different temperature—either 2°C cooler or 2°C warmer. That will possibly induce the fish to spawn. A slight change in the pH also can help. A few drops of phosphoric acid will drop the pH. This of course must be done carefully, accompanied by monitoring with a pH measuring instrument.

SUCCESSFUL BREEDING

A pair of turquoise discus spawning. The male, in the lower photo, is picking off the white eggs which were either unfertilized or died during the early developmental process.

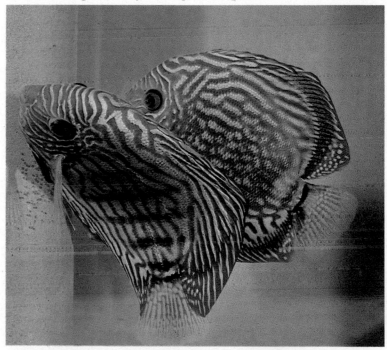

One of the main problems in breeding discus is that the eggs frequently become fungused. This happens to many breeders, and it can ruin their whole enjoyment of keeping discus. Recent thought on the matter is that the mineral deficiency of our water is to blame for fungused eggs. Ion exchange removes all mineral salts, thus keeping the water abnormally poor in minerals. A supplement of those elements can provide the most important trace substances and keep the eggs from succumbing to the fungus. I used a combination trace element product designed for use in marine aquariums and found it to be a remarkable way to counter fungused discus

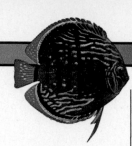

With a really good spawning pair, the male fertilizes the eggs over and over again, even while the female is still laying eggs! Some breeders lay their eggs fairly close together, others spread them out a bit as can be seen here.

eggs. Test by using only a very small quantity.

Access to the parental skin secretion is a decisive factor in rearing the fry. Up to now, if the discus parents were deficient in skin secretion, the young would always be lost. Jack Wattley introduced a hotly debated yolk powder recipe into the discussion of artificial breeding. Then a food originally made for the invertebrates in marine aquaria permitted a decisive breakthrough. With its Aquabiofood U nutrient solution in ampules, the German firm "ab" marketed a liquid food which allowed the artificial breeding of discus to succeed.

The ideal, of course, is for the discus parents to produce their skin secretion and lead their young. Then you can blow that outstanding food out over the school of young discus, and you'll see how they all grow uniformly. There are normally a few young fish in every brood that are retarded in their growth. This won't happen anymore once Aquabiofood is added to the feed.

This liquid food can be loaded easily into a

plastic syringe for convenient dosing. Many breeders now use this food as a standard supplement during the first weeks. I'm now working on a rearing food for discus that can fully utilize the parental skin secretion. Then all the mumbo-jumbo secrecy and mysterious diets will give way to the rearing of valuable young discus. Even that amount of progress still shouldn't turn discus breeding into a mass production, but at least it should help protect breeding populations.

The eggs are guarded by the parents until they hatch. White eggs, indicating dead eggs, are carefully eaten by the parents. The newly hatched fry are zealously guarded, with dead or dying fry eaten in the same manner as bad eggs.

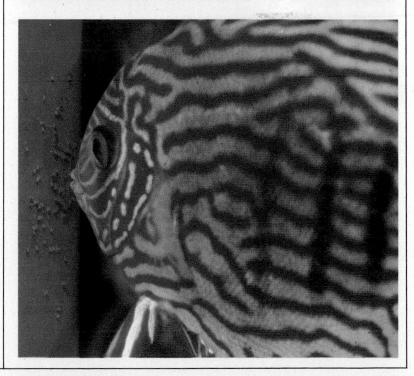

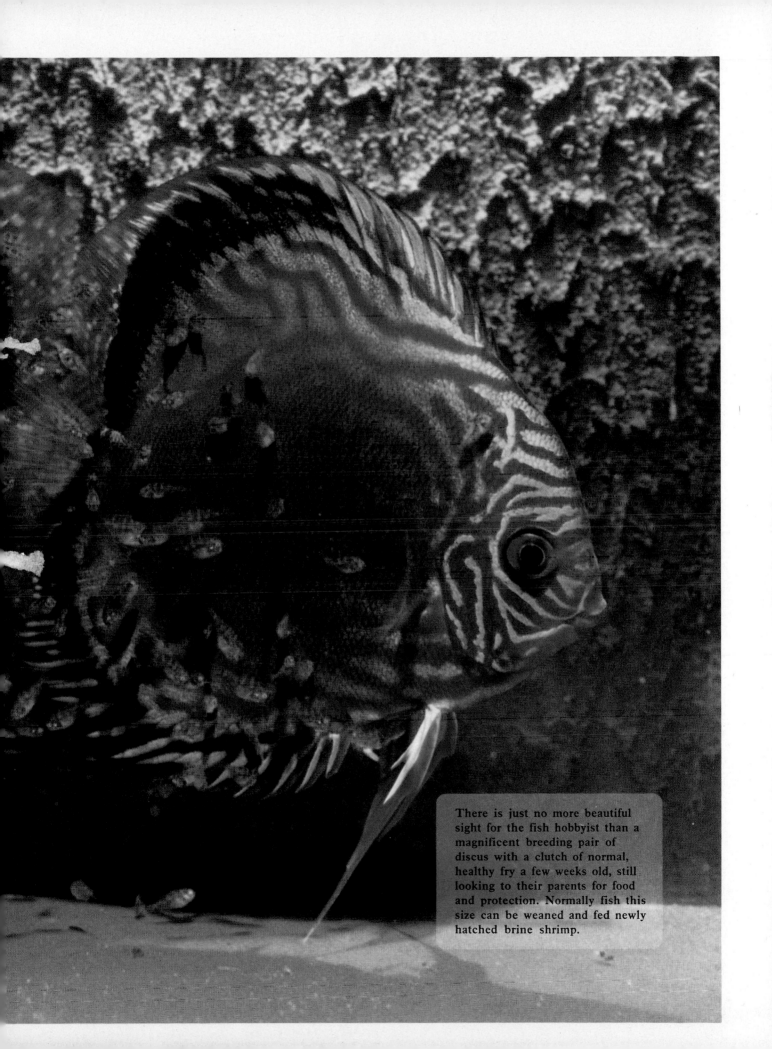

There is just no more beautiful sight for the fish hobbyist than a magnificent breeding pair of discus with a clutch of normal, healthy fry a few weeks old, still looking to their parents for food and protection. Normally fish this size can be weaned and fed newly hatched brine shrimp.

A closeup of a female turquoise discus protecting her two day old fry. The young still have sticky head glands by which they adhere to the spawning site.

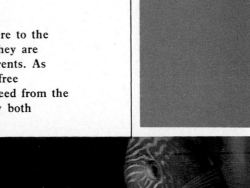

The baby discus adhere to the spawning site while they are protected by their parents. As soon as they become free swimming, they will feed from the body slime exuded by both parents.

Proper and Varied Diet

The quantity of food they eat is as important to discus as it is to us human beings. The quality of the food is important, too. Discus enthusiasts are generally familiar with the slogan "feed several times a day." I'd like to add that, for young fish, "Feed as often daily as possible." WHAT THE YOUNG DISCUS DOES WITHOUT IN THE BEGINNING CAN NEVER BE MADE UP LATER.

Since the discus is a fish that is usually kept in groups in our tanks, special attention must be paid to the weaker ones, for they are always at a disadvantage during feeding. Abundant as well as regular feedings will assure the uniform growth of all young fish in the school.

The baby discus parasitize the parents by eating their parents' slime covering. They comb the entire fish for slime and a large brood, like the one shown here, will grow rapidly for the first few weeks of their lives just eating the slime.

Variety is the trump card. Don't make the mistake of feeding your discus only one kind of food. Give them a full menu to guarantee good nutrition.

Start with high-value flake food, then change over to freeze-dried insect larvae, and then on to beef heart.

Yes, that's what I'm saying: flake food for discus. I'll go even further by recommending food tablets. You'll soon see why.

Back to the flakes. Since there once were no high-value flake varieties available, it was certainly no easy matter to get discus to eat flake foods. Today, however, there are flakes which are just as if they were made for discus, particularly ideally large flakes, so that feeding discus with it can be recommended. These foods provide our fish with very many amino acids, essential fatty acids and roughage for the intestinal tract, as well as vital minerals and vitamins, all of which we weren't able to feed them before at this concentration.

Don't think that discus won't get accustomed to flake food. It's no problem at all to start young fish on these tasty morsels,

Modern processing facilities and state-of-the-art equipment are required to prevent the inclusion of heavy metals in flake foods. Photo courtesy Wardley Products Co.

The new pellet foods are eagerly taken by discus and are much less expensive than the flake foods, besides being less likely to pollute the tank. Flake foods are too dusty and the discus will not eat these fine dust-like particles of flake food.

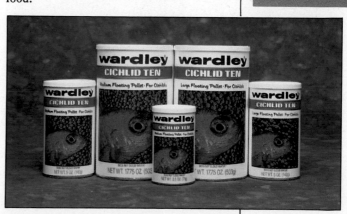

The author prepares his own discus food based on turkey heart with a special formula for other ingredients. His food is the best-selling such food in Europe. Degen rejects some flake foods because their heavy metal content is detrimental to the health of his discus. His food is ground and flash frozen. It is then put into small plastic trays as shown here.

The author also makes tablets, shown below, which contain various foods. Medicines can easily be added to these tablets when necessary.

and you can buy it in all sizes. Once the fish get used to the flakes, they'll always gladly accept them. It's a good feeling to have adult fish that eat their large daily ration of large flakes, which makes feeding them very easy. It often happens that the fish even prefer the large flakes to other food.

I've always seen a different—but important—role for the food tablets. It's a real pleasure to watch a brood of young discus that have just eluded their parents eating food tablets at the side of the tank, up against the glass. You'll grab for your camera to record the experience.

Besides providing a simple way to feed discus, these excellent tablets play yet another quite important role. In the chapter on the control of the worst diseases of discus, I'll share with you a valuable tip on how to use these tablets and medication to rapidly cure sick fish.

Once discus are accustomed to commercial dry foods there will not be any more problems. So consider it very important to accustom small fish to dry food quite early. I've even gotten my wild-caught fish used to flake and tablet foods. That's not hard if you keep wild-caught individuals with other discus that are already used to eating these foods. They'll find the food fast in their competitive urge to get their share.

Beef heart plays another large role in discus diet—a bacteria-free food, hence a solid component of the menu. Buy a large amount, clean off the fat and tendons and slice it into 3 × 3 cm strips. Freeze it. When you need it, remove it from the freezer and let the strips soften

There are at least six major food manufacturers, all offering something 'special'. Try all of them. In this way you have a better chance of giving your fish a well-rounded diet.

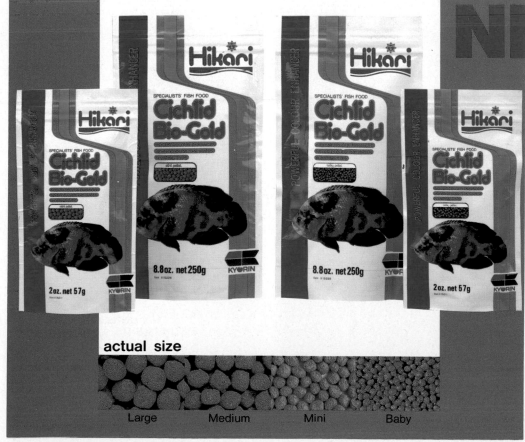

actual size

Large   Medium   Mini   Baby

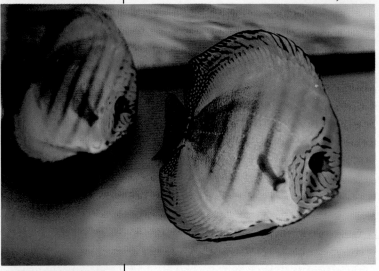

The two pairs of discus on this page and the discus on the facing page were all on display at the discus competition held in Singapore Aquarama in 1989. These were all large fish which sold for high prices at the show. Normally only small discus are shipped from Singapore.

magazines. Breeding of these little white worms naturally requires some care, and a slight odor problem is a possibility.

I accustomed my fish to a morning feeding with the food they don't take too fondly, then for the day I select a food that any household member who stays home can dispense, and at night I feed them what they like and will eat up quickly.

Adult discus should feed at least twice, better three or four times, daily. Try to feed young fish four to six times daily. For this, flakes and tablets have the enormous advantage of convenience. You soon get used to dropping in a food tablet for the little ones whenever you pass by the tank.

I developed the following method of giving supplemental vitamins and growth-promoting substances: I sprinkle the supplemental substance on the food tablets and let it soak in, preferably overnight, then feed the discus with this concentrated supplement and food. Dropping vitamins into the tank water is not effective, since the water dilutes them greatly. The drops I use are manufactured in Germany by the Bayer chemical firm. They're sold under the name Vigantol; perhaps they or their equivalent is available elsewhere as well.

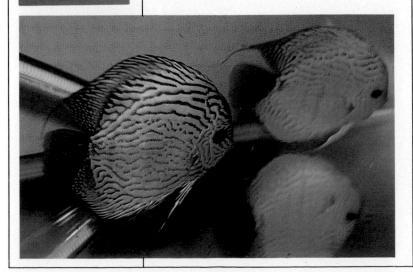

Right: Singapore discus.

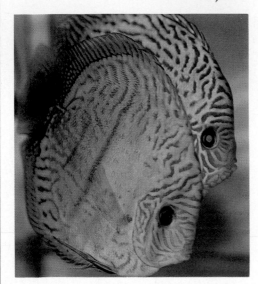

Center: The Chinese red turquoise with young feeding from her body.

Below: Rather poor quality turquoise, by today's standards.

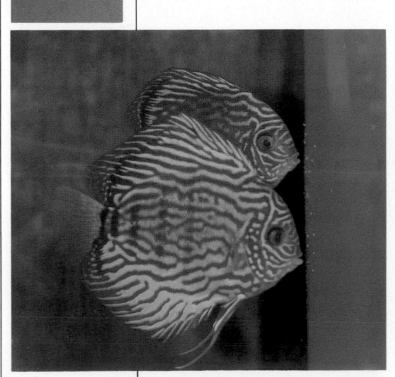

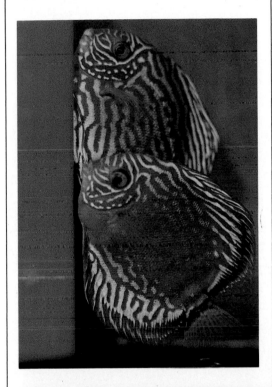

Discus Health

Discus are normally not any more susceptible to disease than other fish, but imagination can lead to all kinds of suppositions. No sooner does a discus apparently swallow the wrong way than the search is on for gill parasites and the water gets loaded with medications. When disease is suspected, first observe the tank carefully. Can the water have been fouled in some way? Is the pH right?— and so on.

The aquarist is advised to keep discus in somewhat hard water, at almost 10°DH, because at that level of hardness the system is more likely to stay in balance than with a very soft water. If you suspect disease, change the water first, but let the new water be as similar as possible to the old. The addition of vitamins also can improve things.

The female is a blue discus, *Symphysodon aequifasciata haraldi*, and her mate is a turquoise. This cross works very well and produces many interesting color variations, the best of which should be inbred, brother-to-sister.

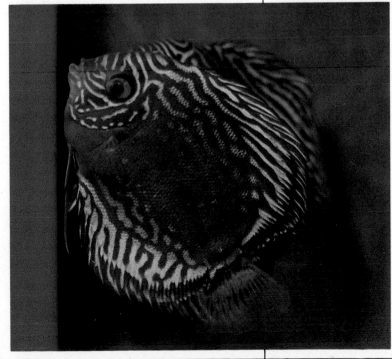

EXPERIENCE FROM HUMAN MEDICINE

Human medications play a role in discus aquaristics, where they can quickly cure discus of serious, life-threatening diseases. Our discus often fall victim to parasites like flagellates or tapeworms. Medications like the German Clont and Simplotan, which are used for trichomonal infections in man, are available, but only as prescription drugs. Up to now, a dosage of 4 mg Clont per liter of water or 1 gram Simplotan tablets per 100 liters was recommended. But because absorption is poor in water, I've developed this method:

Crush finely one Simplotan or two Clont tablets and mix with six crumbled food tablets. Carefully add a few drops of water to make a paste, then coat ten food tablets with it and let them dry overnight. Now, feed these as usual. I've given this laced food regularly as a preventive about once a month on two successive days. If the fish don't eat any more, they can't be saved. So I developed yet another, very effective method:

A pair of 1980 quality turquoise discus showing a ballet of colors.

I grind a Simplotan or Clont tablet very finely and dissolve it in 10 ml water, using an empty, well cleaned bottle from some cold or sniffles remedy, and aspirate it out with a plastic syringe (without any needle). Then I catch the patient, who is placed upon a moist towel and covered, then carefully held quiet and fed with the syringe (without going into the fish's mouth too far with the dull nub of the syringe). At every feeding, once a day, the patient receives 2 ml of the medication. Allow time, for a fish swallows very poorly. After this personalized feeding, wait thirty seconds for the fish to swallow again before returning it to the water. If you don't it will spit out part of the medication once back in its tank. Repeat this procedure for five days in a row. Nothing will happen to the fish. The medication won't hurt them. This treatment normally suffices for the fish to start eating again. You can easily go through the procedure again after a week's rest, if necessary. That's how I saved the lives of discus that stopped eating. Not one single fish was lost with this treatment.

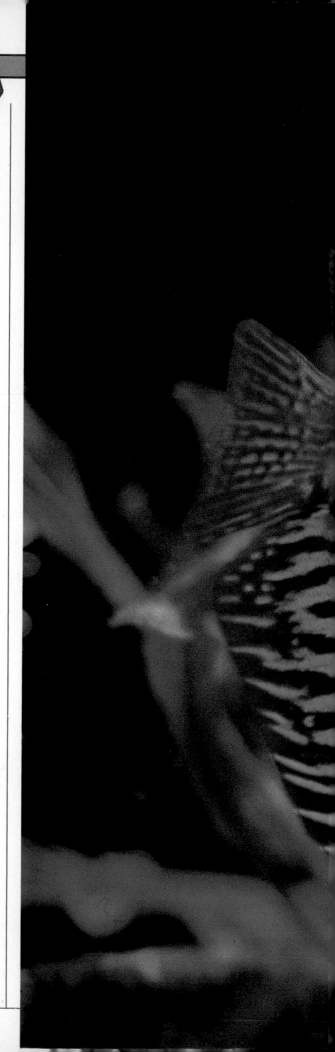

An enhanced *Symphysodon discus discus.* This color variety was called the 'Tarzoo' in the 1970's.

There are medications, though not made especially for discus breeders, which are effective. The table below gives recommendations for the usual, proven drugs (which require a prescription):

Profitability of Breeding Discus You've no doubt already thought of raising discus commercially. And why not? There are, of course, a few prerequisites. First, you've got to know that breeding and caring for discus are very demanding. When you suddenly find yourself with five, six or more tankfuls of discus to care for, it can all turn into just plain *work.* Second, you've got to expect setbacks over the long term, which could ruin your enthusiasm for breeding and third, there's the cost.

Make it a rule to breed only the best specimens and, to start, pick a definite coloration to work with, such as striped

SYMPTOMS	CAUSE	TREATMENT
Choking, belabored respiration, nervous dashing around the tank	Gillworms, parasitic crustaceans (copepods, etc.)	Short bath in Masoten or Neguvon under close supervision, with 10 mg/10 liters water. Repeat in 6 days
Refusal to eat, gelatinous fecal threads	Roundworms, intestinal disease	Long bath with Masoten or Neguvon, with 35 mg/100 liters water, for 4 days. Change ¼ the water daily, then adjust dosage in the tank
Dirty water, long fecal threads	Tapeworms and flukes (trematodes)	Droncit and Mansonil on the food tablets at 20 mg per 10 food tablets.
Poor appetite, very dark color, gelatinous feces, "hole" disease	Flagellates *(Hexamita, Octomitus, Spironucleus)*	Long bath with Clont, 1 tablet per 60 liters water. Long bath with Simplotan, 1 gram tablet per 100 liters water, *or* as described earlier, with food tablet.

turquoise. The important thing here is to be able to regularly deliver a uniform quality of fish over a long period. You'll eventually have to deal with wholesalers, because the pet shops will be able to take only a few young discus off your hands.

Depending upon size and quality, you can get a nice price for a discus that's six to eight weeks old and 3 to 4 cm (about 1⅕ to 1½″) across. That's for turquoise, of course. This applies to lots of 100 fish and more. Smaller lots go for lesser rates.

You'll be asked for a bill and/or receipt—and it's then you realize that you have to start doing things on a businesslike basis, for tax purposes if for no other reason. If you seriously pursue discus breeding, and also are somewhat lucky, your enterprise will be rewarding. Calculate your costs, including your time, and plan your steps. The most critical factor, however, is that the whole thing be fun for you. If you love all this work, and the rewards, then it'll be a beautiful endeavor.

A school of young 7-month-old German discus. They are a bit old for schooling. Normally by this time they separate and go their own way.

The Outlook for Discus

Fortunately for the discus fishes, they can be bred in captivity and greatly improved in coloration. Serious breeders have succeeded in fixing certain natural attributes and maintaining them genetically. We hope that the breeding of fish in captivity will reduce the number of wild ones taken from their native habitats. The practical aquarist thus has an opportunity to help in conservation of our natural resources. It's important to fix, genetically, the color lines and, above all, the good shape of our discus. Avoid breeding elongated bodies and unnaturally long fins. Aquarists are called upon to set up quality standards for the discus.

Discus are being bred in many color varieties. Not all are turquoise, metallic or mottled. The latest objective is for a black discus. Some breeders are inbreeding to make the discus darker and darker. I don't think that a black discus can be achieved in stages. A black mutant will have to appear and then be inbred for generations, increasing an already black area.

Photographic Tips for Discus Enthusiasts

You want to take pictures of your beautiful discus. Here are a few simple, useful tips, but we won't go too deeply into any specialized photography.

I hope you have a reflex camera, which is much better than my pocket and disk cameras; my results with those are unsatisfactory. Then you need a flash unit, preferably with an extension cable, which you can buy inexpensively in a camera shop.

Lenses include the regular 50 mm, an 80- to 135-mm telephoto, and a 35-mm wide-angle. The speed of the lens is unimportant, because we're using flash.

Film for color slides is good to use. Buy a good quality film with at least a rating of 21° DIN (= 100 ASA). Don't use a film faster than 27° DIN (= 400 ASA), because that's where the film starts to get grainy. Slides (transparencies) can be projected, and prints can be made from them. Negative color film

Discus are easy to photograph because they are large and thus they do not require macro lenses to capture their beauty on film. Their light colors also make them more visible when viewing them through the lens.

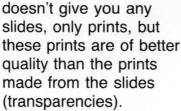

A blue turquoise is when there is more blue and the stripes are red; the red turquoise is when the stripes are blue and the background color is red.

doesn't give you any slides, only prints, but these prints are of better quality than the prints made from the slides (transparencies).

Now let's shoot some pictures. Never shoot frontally into the glass pane. Always shoot at an angle to the glass, with the flash to the left or to the right of the camera. Another way is to lay the flash up against the glass pane and trigger it via an extension cable back to the camera. That gives fewer reflections and shadows.

A polarizing filter over the lens reduces reflections from the glass. Though this filter requires opening up one stop, that's no problem.

Shoot a test roll, recording the setting for each exposure, and then you'll have a guide. Here are several exposures to start you off (flash at least guide number 21):

Film speed 21 DIN (=100 ASA), up to 1 meter from the tank, f/8-f/11. Open up one stop larger when using the polarization filter.

Film speed 27 DIN (=400 ASA), up to 1 meter from the tank, f/16-f/22. Open up one stop larger when using the polarization filter.